Cook Memorial Public Library

3 1122 01538 0442

MAY 0 8 2019

W9-AHH-020

FEATS of 21st-CENTURY ENGINEERING

21st-CENTURY
SHIPS

Enslow Publishing
101 W. 23rd Street
Suite 240
New York, NY 10011
USA

enslow.com

Philip Wolny

COOK MEMORIAL LIBRARY DISTRICT
413 N. MILWAUKEE AVE.
LIBERTYVILLE, ILLINOIS 60048

Published in 2019 by Enslow Publishing, LLC.
101 W. 23rd Street, Suite 240, New York, NY 10011

Copyright © 2019 by Enslow Publishing, LLC.

All rights reserved.

No part of this book may be reproduced by any means without the written permission of the publisher.

Library of Congress Cataloging-in-Publication Data

Names: Wolny, Philip, author.
Title: 21st century ships / Philip Wolny.
Other titles: Twenty-first century ships
Description: New York, NY : Enslow Publishing, LLC., 2019 | Series: Feats of 21st century engineering | Audience: Grades 3-6 |Includes bibliographical references and index. |
Identifiers: LCCN 2017051685| ISBN 9780766097001 (library bound) | ISBN 9780766097018 (pbk.)
Subjects: LCSH: Ships—Juvenile literature. | Ships—History—Juvenile literature.
Classification: LCC VM150 .W65 2018 | DDC 623.82—dc23
LC record available at https://lccn.loc.gov/2017051685

Printed in the United States of America

To Our Readers: We have done our best to make sure all website addresses in this book were active and appropriate when we went to press. However, the author and the publisher have no control over and assume no liability for the material available on those websites or on any websites they may link to. Any comments or suggestions can be sent by e-mail to customerservice@enslow.com.

Photo Credits: Cover, p. 1 (technical drawing) pluie_r/Shutterstock.com; cover, p. 1 (cruise ship) Viktor Hladchenko/Shutterstock.com; p. 4 Magnifier/Shutterstock .com; pp. 6–7 Bloomberg/Getty Images; p. 9 Studio 37/Shutterstock.com; p. 10 Xavier ROSSI/Gamma-Rapho/Getty Images; p. 13 Izz Hazel/Shutterstock.com; p. 15 Print Collector/Hulton Archive/Getty Images; pp. 16–17 Roger Clark ARPS/ Shutterstock.com; p. 19 Fanthomme Hubert/Paris Match Archive/Getty Images; p. 22 Kanok Sulaiman/Shutterstock.com; p. 23 Chris Wilkins/AFP/Getty Images; pp. 24–25 Zhang peijian Imaginechina/AP; pp. 28–29 Faraways/Shutterstock .com; p. 30 Corine van Kapel/Shutterstock.com; p. 33 U.S. Navy/Getty Images; p. 35 Getty Images; p. 38 Bertrand Guay/Getty Images; p. 41 Lev Fedoseyev/ TASS/Getty Images.

CONTENTS

Engineers have found ways to improve the speed, carrying capacity, and efficiency of twenty-first-century ships.

Introduction

On a Sunday in the spring of 2016, the MS *Harmony of the Seas* began its career on the oceans and seas of the world. Its maiden voyage—known also as an inaugural voyage—took it from Southampton, England, to Barcelona, Spain. It is a cruise ship, a type of passenger ship used for vacation and relaxation. Cruise ships also often take their passengers to different ports for tourism and leisure.

But the *Harmony* is no ordinary ship. It is actually the largest passenger cruise ship to ever sail the seas. For now, it still lays claim to the title of biggest boat of its kind. Can you imagine how much metal, wiring, and other materials were needed for its construction? Consider the knowledge required to design it and the money needed to build it. None of it would be possible without the advanced engineering we now have available at our fingertips in the twenty-first century.

Ships are important because they move things and people around the world. Many other industries would not exist without ships. Meanwhile, the world's militaries rely on ships to defend their nations. Coast guards also use boats to do their jobs, including rescuing people. Other ships are useful for scientific missions. Still others carry people, whether they are cruise-ship tourists or commuters who take many of the thousands of ferries nationwide.

Cruise ships dock at the piers of the Port of Genoa in Italy. Genoa is a major port on the Mediterranean Sea.

It may seem that records are broken almost annually for the biggest cruise ship. Such boats are getting longer and taller. They are carrying more people and crew. Other kinds of ships, like oil tankers, are also getting more massive by the year. This is because engineers are designing more creative and advanced ships. Shipbuilders use new techniques and materials, too. The demand for bigger and better ships grows. Businesspeople who run shipping companies want more fuel-efficient vessels that can carry larger loads. Cruise line companies love to launch ever more impressive cruise ships. There is certainly something about such incredible feats of engineering that captures the imagination. Land vehicles can get only so big, but boats have been increasing in size throughout the decades.

Ships age and break down. New ones must be built every year as older ones are decommissioned, or retired. Since the turn of the century, ships of all kinds are bigger, better, faster, and more efficient. The twenty-first century will bring even more astounding examples of maritime (sea-related) construction.

Big Ships, Big Jobs

Traveling on the seas has been an important human activity for thousands of years. For most of history, ships were the only way to cross long distances on water. Even now, in the age of aircraft, big ships remain incredibly important. There are many kinds of ships, and they do many different kinds of jobs. Ships are designed and engineered to make sure they can do these different jobs well. Before anything, they must be built to be seaworthy. This means they have to be constructed to sail safely on the water for long periods of time. The biggest vessels need much planning and work before they can even be tested on open water.

From Idea to Ship

Shipbuilding is an incredible process. It starts with basic designs and engineering plans. Nowadays, these usually are done using computer-aided design (CAD). These designs make the difference between ships that are seaworthy versus those that sink or otherwise fail. People who design and build ships are sometimes known as naval architects. Just as land architects oversee the process of making buildings, naval architects oversee shipbuilding.

Once a ship is built, it is launched into the water for testing. Then it is transported to its owners.

Once a ship's designs are approved, the next stage is production planning. Big companies, including car companies like Hyundai and Mitsubishi, manufacture most large vessels. The production process includes many different people. That's why it has to be led by one or more project managers. Plans are often reviewed and revised many times. Many others contribute their knowledge.

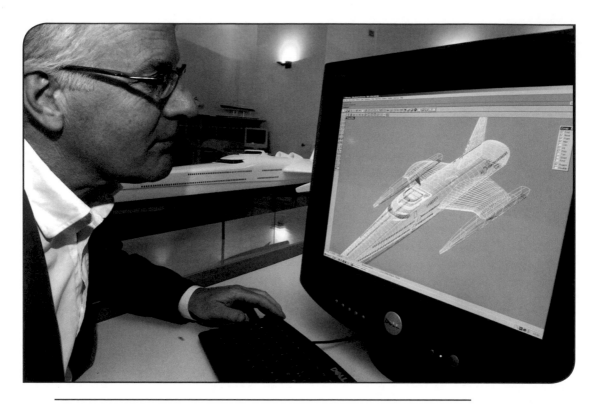

Naval architects work on designs for ships in many stages. It takes a long time to design and build something as massive as a ship!

With plans finalized, shipbuilders prepare a facility for the new construction. This construction usually takes place at a shipyard. For very big craft, the shipbuilders use steel to build most or all of the outside of the ship. The outside of the ship is called the hull.

Before construction, the steel must be pretreated with chemicals. These help prevent the iron that makes up most of steel from weakening and turning into rust. This process is called corrosion.

After the steel is treated to prevent corrosion, workers run giant machines to turn the steel into smaller sheets. They then process these sheets. Other machines are used to roll sheets of steel into the shapes needed to build the hull and other parts of the ship.

Other machines are used to build the hull blocks. Still other machines build the structures that will fill the inside of the ship itself. A lot of machines are used in the building of a ship!

Workers fit pipes and other equipment within the blocks. These pipes will serve the same functions on the ship that blood vessels and other organs serve in a human body. The workers assemble big blocks of the hull in a carefully planned order on a shipbuilding dock.

Traditionally, workers lay down the keel. Many shipbuilding companies even celebrate with a special ceremony to mark this important milestone.

Once everything is put together, it is time to test the ship's seaworthiness. This means the ship is placed in the water to see if it floats without any problems. If the ship is deemed seaworthy, the shipbuilding facility delivers it to the owners that commissioned, or ordered, it. Then it is ready to sail the seas and move people or goods around the world.

Long Ships in History

Each era has its own gigantic seacraft. In the early twentieth century, the schooner *Wyoming* was the longest and largest wooden ship ever constructed, at 450 feet (140 meters). At 883 feet (269 m), the RMS *Titanic* was the biggest ship of its time before an iceberg sank it in the Atlantic Ocean on its maiden voyage in 1912. The longest ship ever built was the oil supertanker known as the *Seawise Giant*, with a length of 1,504 feet (458 m). It was scrapped (taken out of service and broken down into scrap metal) in 2010.

Ocean Liners, Tanker, Destroyers, and More

Today, there are many kinds of big ships sailing the seas. Some are passenger vessels. These big boats, like cruise ships and ferries, carry large numbers of people. A cruise ship is like a giant floating hotel. Its staff must be very big to handle the hundreds or even thousands of guests it holds. Others, like oil tankers and container ships that carry cargo, have smaller crews. Tanker design has to account for the way that oil and other liquid cargo moves back and forth in transit. Meanwhile, container ships and other cargo vessels have to be able to handle huge differences in weight.

Each kind of ship might be designed in a slightly different way. The differences are important because carrying oil and carrying 1,500 human passengers are two completely different jobs. A warship will have ultra-thin armor on it to protect against attack but not enough to slow it down. Some ships may even be designed for certain sea routes. For example, certain tankers are too big to make it through important canals, like the Suez Canal connecting the Persian Gulf with the Mediterranean Sea.

What Makes Ships Float?

Scientists have studied how water behaves for thousands of years. In the Western world, it was the Greek mathematician Archimedes who is credited with writing about the concept of buoyancy around 250 BCE. Buoyancy is the force that a fluid has as it pushes up against something that has been placed in it. For example, Archimedes claimed that he experimented by dropping a crown in water. He then calculated how much water was displaced, or moved, by that crown. Try to pick up a heavy object (or person!) underwater. You will notice

Shipbuilding is one of the biggest global industries. A vessel is shown here on a floating dry dock in Port Klang, Malaysia.

it feels lighter than it would on dry land. This is because the buoyant force of the water is helping you a bit.

The more a boat weighs, the more it tends to sink in the water. When the boat weighs less than the greatest amount of water it will displace, or push, it will float. The weight of the boat creates a force, but usually the amount of pushback from the water below (called upthrust) will equal that force. These forces are equal until the boat passes the maximum weight. Then it sinks.

Cruise Ships: All Aboard!

If you have ever seen a cruise ship, you have probably gotten a sense of how big they are. Not long ago, there was not really a cruise ship industry. Instead, boats of that size were known as ocean liners. Such ships were used for transatlantic voyages, usually crossing between Europe and the Americas. They were built with reinforced steel to meet any challenge on the high seas. The bow, or front of the ship, was tapered. This helped the liner to cut through high or heavy waves.

Eventually, the ocean liner industry declined. This was because airplanes were much quicker and more efficient. A trip that used to take several weeks in a big boat could now be made in less than ten hours by plane.

Cruise ships became popular in the 1960s as a luxury vacation option. These ships would take people to and from the same port, often visiting other ports on the way during a trip of several days. Cruise ships began to look different from their older ocean liner cousins. The newer ships did not have to be prepared for possibly harsh conditions over several weeks of travel. The bows became shorter and wider than before. After all, they would not face stormy seas as often. While cruise ships were still long, they were more

T.S.S. *Aquitania*

Length, 901 ft.
Width, 97 ft.
Tonnage, 47,000.
Speed, 23 Knots.

This artist's rendition shows the ocean liner known as the RMS *Aquitania*, launched in 1914, which moved transatlantic passengers. During World Wars I and II, the *Aquitania* transported Allied troops.

boxlike and not as thin. This let them carry even more passengers. They were also slower than the liners of the early twentieth century.

It is only in recent years that newly designed cruise ships have begun to look a bit like much older ocean liners. Some newer cruise ships go faster, like the original ocean liners that depended on their speed to transport passengers more quickly. Modern cruise ships are among the largest vessels ever constructed. They are also some of the most technologically advanced.

The impressive cruise ship *Harmony of the Seas* embarked on its maiden voyage from Southampton, England, on May 22, 2016.

Keeping It Stable

Big ships need to be pretty stable in the water. Cruise ships almost always have something called a displacement hull. Its shape looks like a big rectangle with round edges. Ships with displacement hulls move slowly, however. They move so slowly that even running engines at full speed gets the fastest cruise ship to only about 30 knots, the accepted measure of boat speed on water. At 35 miles (56 kilometers) per hour, the speed is not fast. Passengers on a cruise ship almost never feel it rocking or moving side to side.

The *Harmony of the Seas*

In service since 2016, the *Harmony of the Seas* is the largest of a series of huge cruise ships known as the Oasis class, owned by Royal Caribbean International. These are the largest passenger ships on Earth, and the *Harmony* is the biggest of these. Ship size is often judged by gross tonnage (GT), and the *Harmony* measures a staggering 226,963 GT. It boasts a length of 1,881 feet (362 m). The beam of the ship—its widest point at the waterline, where the hull meets the water—is about 154 feet (46.9 m). With sixteen passenger decks, the boat can accommodate a maximum of 6,870 people. A crew of 2,300 is required to run it. It is like a small floating city.

A ship of this size needs plenty of power in the engine room to move it. Its three ABB Azipod thrusters, which push the ship along underwater, use what are basically giant propellers. Each is powered by an electric drive motor located in a pod outside the actual hull. Additional thrusters—sometimes known as tunnel thrusters—are usually built into the bow or stern of the ship. These help ships like *Harmony* maneuver, especially when doing trickier moves, like docking into a port.

Even more power is needed to power the rest of the ship. The *Harmony* has three diesel fuel engines that can produce 18,860 kilowatts each and three smaller ones creating 13,860 kilowatts apiece. For comparison, an average apartment resident might use 500–800 kilowatts per month. This power is delivered through about 3,300 miles (5,311 km) of electrical wire laid out throughout the ship. Water and wastewater run through a pipe system that totals about 150 miles (241 km).

Diesel engines are shown in the large engine room of the *MSC Fantasia*, an Italian cruise boat that is the flagship vessel of the MSC company.

A Greener Cruise Ship

The *Harmony of the Seas* actually uses about 20 percent less power than earlier models in the Oasis class, according to Royal Caribbean's website. This is impressive because some of these ships already were efficient to begin with. Some of its "green" features include the following:

- Air bubbles that are naturally forced out of the hull help the ship ride more easily through the water.
- Better insulation keeps heat and air-conditioning in, and outside heat or cold out.
- Heat created by the engines powers steam generators, creating more heat.
- Self-cleaning systems in the engines called gas scrubbers get rid of up to 98 percent of some kinds of dangerous air-polluting gases.
- Light-emitting diodes (LEDs) are installed all over the ship. LED lights use less energy, work for much longer, and are believed to be safer for the environment when thrown away.

Years ago, few people could have imagined boats that would reach many stories high and would be able to carry thousands of passengers. New technologies being developed now, and ones we can barely imagine, will make even more incredible ships possible. Modern engineers imagine super-strong alloys, or combinations of steel and other metals, that are also super lightweight. Those who care about the environment believe that some cruise ships may be run mostly or entirely on solar power, wind turbines, or some combination of the two. Some people picture cruise ships getting bigger and bigger until they actually do resemble cities floating around the world. In a way, they would be their own ports.

Tankers: Fueling the Coming Century

Cruise ships may capture the imagination because most people can imagine riding on one. They have also been the subjects of films, like the 1997 blockbuster *Titanic*. But there are even bigger ships that the average person will never set foot on, unless they work for an energy company. Those ships are tankers.

A Different Kind of Ship

Tankers are designed to move large amounts of oil, gas, coal, or similar materials. Just as cruise ships are designed in certain ways to hold passengers, tankers need to be constructed to transport these natural resources. They have to be able to transport them safely, too. A minor fire can cause an explosion. Meanwhile, a breach (a break or hole) in the hull can cause oil or other hazardous material to spill out. Even small oil spills can cause terrible environmental damage to oceans and coastal areas, including killing large numbers of marine life.

Like other kinds of big ships, oil tankers have been increasing in size for decades. This is so they can transport greater volumes of

An oil tanker is shown docked near an oil rig. Such tankers keep the world supplied with fuel from major oil-producing regions, such as the Persian Gulf and the Gulf of Mexico.

oil. Making fewer trips is more efficient, leading to lower costs. Oil companies might own their own tankers, but many of them hire the services of independent boats and fleets. Since technology has made it possible, these boats have grown ever bigger. Despite their size, tankers and other cargo vessels have relatively small crews. This is because they are set up very simply. Mostly, they have one or several giant compartments.

The threat of oil spills, like the 1989 *Exxon Valdez* disaster, led to passage of laws to make tankers safer. For example, by 2015, all tankers in US waters were required to have a double hull. Like an inner tube inside a car tire, this design helps lessen the risk of major spills. If a breach occurs, the "hull within a hull" at least provides a second line of defense.

Vessels skimmed oil off the surface of Prince William Sound, off the Alaskan coast, to help clean up the massive *Exxon Valdez* spill of 1989.

Giants of the Ocean

In the twentieth century, tankers jumped in size in the decade from the 1960s to the 1970s. Naval architects of the last few decades have been able to use design software and other technologies to solve shipbuilding problems quickly. These tools also made it easier to efficiently engineer these particular ocean giants.

This century's tankers used deadweight tonnage, or DWT, as a way to classify their size. This refers to how much the ship can carry. Tankers have gotten so big that the largest modern vessels are called supertankers. These are split into two groups: Very Large Crude Carriers (VLCC), which can move from 180,000 to 320,000 DWT, and Ultra Large Crude Carriers (ULCC), which range in size between 320,000 to 500,000 DWT. They are the world's largest shipping vessels. The "Crude" refers to crude oil, the kind of oil found underground and in the oceans, before it has been changed, or processed, into gasoline fuels.

Some of the largest supertankers operating today are four ships built by the company Tankers International in 2002 and 2003: *TI Africa*, *TI Asia*, *TI Europe*, and *TI Oceania*. These are all 1,247 feet (380 m) long, with 441,585 DWT. They are known for being very quick for

Supertanker *TI Europe* is shown in February 2017 at a berth in the Chinese port of Ningbo, which boasts the largest crude oil terminal in Asia.

Metal, Air, Water . . . and Speed!

A scientist at the University of California, Los Angeles (UCLA) named Chang-Jin Kim is working on technology that would insert a super-small layer of air between the hull of the ship and the ocean water it travels over. This microscopic layer would act almost the way a Teflon coating on a frying pan keeps eggs or other food from sticking to the pan itself. With "drag"—the way the water slows the ship—much reduced, tankers and other vessels like cargo ships might be able to go incredibly fast. Of course, the technology is still a long way from finished.

their size. They can go about 19 miles (30.5 km, or 16.5 knots) per hour. Nowadays, however, when gas prices are high, many big ships go slower to save fuel. When prices are low, companies can afford to sail the tankers faster.

Prelude to the Future

Perhaps the largest man-made machine of all time is also the largest seagoing vessel. Developed and built by the international energy giant Royal Dutch Shell, the *Prelude* FLNG is a mobile natural gas facility. Some people questioned whether *Prelude* can truly be considered a vehicle. It is about 1,588 feet (484 m) long and 239.5 feet (73 m) wide. The facility is equipped with three 6,700-horsepower engines that move it when necessary. In addition, *Prelude* has also been built to withstand a Category 5 hurricane, including winds of at least 157 miles (253 km). It was built for about $12 billion in Geoje, South Korea. In June 2017, it arrived at the Browse Basin off Australia's coast, where it will pump the offshore gas fields.

Container Ships: Moving the World Economy

Over the last twenty years, maritime technology has made shipping part of a truly global economy. Many of the products in our stores and homes are shipped from faraway places. While some items are sent by plane, train, or truck, chances are, many of them got to where they were going in a container on a giant cargo ship.

As their name tells us, bulk carriers transport bulk cargo. This could mean large amounts of grain or other crops, gravel, cement, wood chips, refrigerated goods, animal products, and much more. Such bulk items can be tossed together in large spaces, called holds.

The Biggest Ships on Earth

Another kind of cargo vessel is the container ship. Toward the end of the twentieth century, containerization became the most important way of shipping non-bulk cargo. This means that cargo is placed into standard (same-size) containers. Having a predictable size makes loading and unloading this cargo much quicker. It also requires far fewer human beings on the docks.

A crane unloads a container from a ship in port. Automation and other advances in technology allow more efficient shipping of goods around the world.

Years ago, cargo had to be divided up after being unloaded. Traders kept written records on paper. Shipping companies, and both buyers and sellers of goods, now use computer-automated tracking systems for their cargo. These make it possible to send a container from a factory in China to a Walmart warehouse in the United States without ever having to open it. All containers are given specific numbers and are tracked through their journeys.

Container ships are the largest ships on Earth. Many of those launched since the beginning of the twenty-first century are so big that they can only dock at a small number of ports around the world. Some cannot pass through the Suez or Panama canals. Even many of those that can need special procedures to do so.

The number of containers any specific container ship can hold is measured using twenty-foot equivalent units, or TEU. This refers to the standard shipping container being about 20 feet (6.09 m) long and between 4 feet, 3 inches (129.5 centimeters) and 9.5 feet (2.9 m) tall. Most containers are about 8 feet (2.4 m) wide.

From Enormous to Gargantuan

It seems that hardly a year goes by without another container ship being named the "biggest ship on the high seas." Maersk, the Danish company that is the largest container and cargo operator in the world, introduced its Triple E Class ships in 2013. The *Madrid Maersk* is 1,309 feet (399 m) long, with a maximum TEU of 20,568 and gross tonnage of 214,286.

However, not long after Maersk launched its line, OOCL, a company based in Hong Kong, China, topped it with an even more gargantuan ship, the OOCL *Hong Kong*. According to *Marine Insight*, it can carry up to 21,413 TEU and was the first ship to ever surpass 21,000 TEU. It also beats the Maersk line by a hair, at 1,311.9 feet (399.87 m).

The Maersk E Class ships use as much steel as eight Eiffel Towers. The containers they hold could fill more than thirty mile-long trains or thirty-six thousand cars!

Maersk also says that these ships are the most environmentally friendly container ships ever made. They carry 16 percent more

The OOCL *Hong Kong* makes its maiden call—a ship's first appearance in a port—at Rotterdam, Netherlands, in June 2017. For now, it remains the world's largest container vessel.

Ballast Water

Ballast water is water that is taken into the hull of a ship, helping balance the ship and make it stable. This helps when a ship's weight changes when containers or other cargo are added or removed. Ships can discharge it to get through shallow waters. They might only discharge forward tanks to keep the bow of the ship raised when they hit rough seas. New "ecological" ballast filters and systems remove organisms accidentally sucked up from seawaters. Many invasive species destroy native ones in other ocean areas and in lakes and rivers because they were carried in ballast water.

cargo, even though they are only about 9.8 feet (3 m) longer and wider than previous container vessels the company produced. New engine designs that include reusing engine heat to power other ship systems and limiting the speed of the vessels to 26.4 miles (42.5 km, or 24 knots) will also help. Sailing at half that speed also means tremendous savings in fuel. Of course, fully loaded ships means the ships are working most efficiently.

The Next Era of Shipping

Cargo ships, especially container ships, will not be the only things that will change in the years ahead. Managers of ports and canals are scrambling to accommodate bigger ships. Shipping lanes will have to change, too. The uncertain future that climate change brings will affect how these vessels operate. Shipping lanes formerly blocked by gigantic ice sheets in the Arctic will open up as sea ice melts. Some are predicted to be accessible as early as 2020.

Military Ships: At War on the Water

War ships and other military marine craft have been important parts of national defense for centuries. The US military and others have often been at the cutting edge of new technologies. This has been true not only in terms of weapons systems. The US Navy and other service branches have been pioneers in naval engineering and architecture, too.

There are many kinds of military craft. Among the biggest are aircraft carriers. Destroyers and other craft are smaller but remain incredibly important parts of many navies. These days, the slogan of the maritime military might be "Fight Smarter, Not Harder." Many newer vessels of twenty-first-century fleets owe as much to advanced technologies as they do to overwhelming firepower.

A Floating Base and Airfield

One of the most important weapons of the US Navy is the aircraft carrier. These massive ships do more than just transport personnel and serve as floating airfields. They also allow the military to move large amounts of equipment to conflict zones. The main job of aircraft carriers is to carry fighter jets and other aircraft. Without them, the navy and other services would have to build or use pre-existing airfields on land. The twenty-first-century aircraft carrier has some of the most sophisticated radar and networking technologies available.

One of the newest aircraft carriers in the American fleet is the USS *Gerald R. Ford*, the first of a series of ships with the same name. Because it displaces more than 70,000 tons (71,000 metric tons), it is considered a supercarrier. The *Ford* actually displaces more than 100,000 tons (90,718 metric tons) when fully loaded. It is 1,106 feet (337 m) long.

Boasting the first new aircraft carrier design for the United States in decades, the new USS *Gerald R. Ford* supercarrier takes to the water off the coast of Newport News, Virginia.

Like all the aircraft carriers built by the United States military for some time now, its main power source is not fossil fuel. Rather, it is nuclear-powered. This means that an onboard nuclear facility generates energy. It heats up the steam that powers the turbines that help move the ship. It also powers all the other systems. According to tech website Foxtrot Alpha, the *Ford*'s improved nuclear reactor provides 300 percent more electrical capacity than previous carriers. It will not enter active service for a few years, however.

Massive Manpower

One big difference between military ships and many civilian ones is the number of crew members involved. An oil tanker or container ship may have two or three dozen crew members at most. The giant container ship *Emma Maersk* has a crew of thirteen and room for another seventeen, give or take. An aircraft carrier, however, is a far more complex vessel. The USS *Harry Truman*, for instance, fits approximately 6,250 crew members. Certain automated systems of the *Gerald R. Ford*-class of supercarriers, including a new launch system, mean that they require only 75 percent the crew members of older ships.

From Battleships to Destroyers

Aircraft carriers themselves do not fight directly on the open seas. That job is instead left to naval destroyers. While carriers are bigger and slower, destroyers are swift and maneuverable. Up through 1945—the final year of World War II—larger battleships handled the jobs that destroyers now handle. Besides fighting other battleships at sea, they had so much firepower that they were used to bomb coastlines and other targets.

Huge battleships were too expensive to build, maintain, and crew. Other smaller boats and defense systems could do the job of battleships better and more cheaply. Destroyers got their shortened name from the longer "torpedo boat destroyer." They were smaller and quicker. Destroyers still have sizable crews. For instance, the USS *John S. McCain* (named after the current Arizona senator's father and grandfather, both navy admirals), has just under three hundred crew members.

The US Navy's new hi-tech destroyer, the USS *Zumwalt*, conducts at-sea tests and trials on the Atlantic Ocean. It is the largest destroyer ever built for the navy.

More with Less

But new technologies are allowing the United States military to launch ships that do more with less. For example, the USS *Zumwalt*, the first of its class, was built to be far more efficient. First launched in 2013, it is about 100 feet (30.5 m) longer than most US destroyers currently in service and almost twice the size. However, it also requires a crew about half the size. The *Zumwalt* will be the most technologically sophisticated warship ever to hit the water.

One advantage is that its radar signature is 1/50th of other destroyers. To enemy radar, it looks like a smaller fishing boat. It can thus sneak near enemy shorelines and bomb them. According to *Popular Science*, the ship can get especially close because it "can operate in just 30 feet of water, and … from the shallows, the Zumwalt can then wipe out enemy defenses up to 72 miles [116 km] away." In the old days, sailors had to manually load shells and clear casings from big naval guns. Now, the guns are controlled by a computer in the ship's command center.

Four gas-turbine generators on the *Zumwalt* give it more than ten times the electrical power of similar recent craft. Many of its systems are automated. This makes it possible for the vessel to operate with half the crew twentieth-century destroyers needed.

6

A Greener Future

Energy efficiency and green technologies have become more important than ever before in ship engineering. Tomorrow's ships need better and more efficient power sources. Solar power will probably figure into ship design even more, too. Every little bit counts, since the more ships operate every year, the greater the pollution and impact on the environment.

While looking forward, naval engineers and architects may take some lessons from the past as well. Namely, future ships may actually make more use of wind power. This will include using sails and wind turbines that produce electricity. It is an exciting time for engineers and others involved in creating new, environmentally friendly vessels.

Solar Power

It will probably be a very long time before huge cargo ships or military destroyers can run mostly or entirely on solar power, or energy from the sun. This does not mean that many engineers won't try to include it in their new designs. In 2010, the German company Knierim Yachtbau launched the MS *Tûranor PlanetSolar*. Designed by naval architects LOMOcean Design, this ship is the world's largest solar electric vehicle. It is also the first of its kind to sail itself around the world.

The *PlanetSolar* is covered in 5,780 square feet (537 sq m) of solar panels. Onboard, 8.5 tons (7.7 metric tons) of lithium-ion batteries store the energy the solar panels collect. It is a catamaran, a ship with two hulls, which often is quicker and more aerodynamic. The ship needs as much help as it can get, since it travels pretty slowly (a maximum of 14 knots, or 16 mph/25.7 kph). At 101.7 feet (31 m) long, and a width, or beam, of 49.2 feet (15 m), the ship currently acts as a floating laboratory to study climate change on the seas. The ship's performance will also hopefully help engineers build bigger and faster vehicles that utilize mostly solar power.

The MS *Tûranor PlanetSolar* is shown docked off the Seine River in France in December 2015, showing off its impressive set of solar panels.

"Zero Emissions"

The problem with big ships, even if they are environmentally friendlier now, is emissions. Emissions are the polluting gases released into the atmosphere that affect the climate and the health of all living things. One promising example of a project designed to help solve this problem is being led by Nippon Yusen Kabushiki Kaisha, or NYK. NYK, one of the biggest and oldest shipping companies, is planning the NYK Super Eco Ship 2030 with several partners. Website Techcrunch describes its design as a "vessel straight out of Star Trek."

NYK hopes the ship, which will reach about 1,158 feet (354 m) long, will run mostly on fuel cells using liquefied natural gas (LNG). The rest of its power will come from solar and wind backup systems. Its hull will weigh much less than other current models of container ship. Engineers are also working on a "frictionless hull," according to NYK. The company says the ship will reduce carbon dioxide emissions by 69 percent. The ultimate goal for naval architects and engineers in the twenty-first century is "zero emissions."

Going LNG

According to Haifeng Wang of the International Council on Clean Transportation (ICCT), heavy fuel oil (HFO) has been the main power source for most cargo ships since the 1960s. The International Maritime Organization (IMO) governs international shipping. It declared new rules in 2015 that vessels operating in some major shipping lanes would have to use cleaner fuels. One possible alternative that qualifies is liquefied natural gas (LNG). Critics have long said that LNG can be dangerous due to possible explosions. But companies like Maersk say that newer engine designs that keep engine rooms cooler could make wide LNG use possible and necessary.

The Nuclear Option

There is some controversy about using nuclear energy to power civilian ships. The 2011 Fukushima nuclear disaster in Japan made people especially nervous. Many people believe the negatives of atomic energy are worth it, however. If "dirtier" fossil fuels pollute the environment so badly, there may be little option but to go nuclear.

The first nuclear-powered submarine, the USS *Nautilus*, launched in 1955. According to the World Nuclear Association, more than 140 nuclear-fueled ships are on the seas as of 2017. The main nonmilitary civilian vessels that rely on atomic energy are icebreakers, most of them in the Russian Arctic. A handful of nuclear cargo ships were launched in the 1960s but were too expensive to run at the time. Nuclear power makes sense for these mainly because it is the only power source strong enough to help break the thick ice of the region. Refueling using traditional fuels is also difficult or impossible in such areas. The largest and newest icebreaker of this kind, the *Arktika*, was launched by the Russian Federation in 2016, the first of several of its named class.

The advantage of nuclear ships is that they can run for years on a limited amount of nuclear fuel, like uranium. Besides disposing of nuclear wastes, there is also the risk of meltdowns. Many supporters of nuclear power for shipping say that smaller reactors such as those on ships are far safer than big power plants like Fukushima. According to Clean Technica, there have been no accidents on the ocean involving nuclear naval vessels or icebreakers for decades.

What the Future Holds

There are many technologies besides those that deal directly with fuel that will change shipbuilding in the coming century. This includes those that can really help engineers and architects imagine what

The icebreaker *50 Let Pobedy* (Russian for "50 Years of Victory"), shown here making a path through the Arctic Ocean, is an Arktika-class nuclear vessel.

ships will look like. In 2015, *Marine Insight* reported on how the Naval Surface War Center (NSWC) used 3D printing to construct scale models of a naval hospital ship. Such techniques can save valuable time and help eliminate poor designs.

Automation is another area where shipbuilding and sailing will change. Robots are on track to take over many dangerous and difficult shipyard tasks. *Marine Insight* noted that South Korea's Geoje shipyard makes about thirty ships a year and that 68 percent of its production is carried out with robotic systems.

Robots will also become more common on ships as deckhands and will fill countless other jobs. A cruise in 2030, for example, might be crewed entirely by artificial intelligence. Robots may make up the majority of those loading and unloading cargo ships, fixing engines on the high seas, and much more.

Yet another development that is still being worked out is ballast-free ship design. Many shipping companies and governments seek a solution to the ill effects of ballast water contaminating many regions. Big, open pipes from the bow to the stern in the hull will let a ship's captain control water coming in and out, without keeping any excess water inside the hull.

Whatever inventions and new techniques are used, now is an exciting time for naval architecture and engineering. Whether used to haul the millions of products that fill our stores and the fuels that keep society running, to provide people with fun and recreation, or to defend the shores of many nations, ships of the twenty-first century will be bigger and more advanced and will continue to stir the imagination.

CHRONOLOGY

1912

The RMS *Titanic*, the largest ship of its era, launches and sinks four days into its maiden voyage.

1955

The first nuclear-powered submarine, the USS *Nautilus*, is launched.

1957

Malcolm McLean, the "Father of Containerization," sails the first modern container ship, *Ideal X*.

1958

The USS *Enterprise* is the first nuclear-powered aircraft carrier in the US arsenal.

1979

The longest supertanker in history, *Seawise Giant*, is completed.

2005

Hyundai Heavy Industries' Ulsan Shipyard in South Korea, the world's busiest and biggest shipyard, marks 100 million DWT of production in its lifetime.

2016

Harmony of the Seas is launched as the largest cruise ship in the world.

2017

The USS *Gerald R. Ford,* first of its aircraft carrier class, is commissioned; OOCL *Hong Kong,* the largest container ship ever built, is delivered.

BIBLIOGRAPHY

Blewitt, Laura. "New American Oil Tankers Great for Traders, Lousy for Owners." Bloomberg, August 17, 2017. https://www.bloomberg.com/news/articles/2017-08-17/new-american-oil-tankers-are-great-for-traders-lousy-for-owners.

Dillow, Clay. "The Most Technologically Advanced Warship Ever Built." *Popular Science*, October 16, 2012. https://www.popsci.com/technology/article/2012-08/ocean-power.

D'Orazio, Dante. "An Inside Look at the World's Largest Solar-Powered Boat." The Verge, June 22, 2013. https://www.theverge.com/2013/6/22/4454980/ms-turanor-planetsolar-solar-powered-boat-photo-essay.

Flanagan, Graham. "Scientists Created a Teflon-Like Surface That Could Make Oil Tankers Super Fast." *Business Insider*, January 7, 2015. http://www.businessinsider.com/new-technology-oil-tankers-ucla-2015-1.

Garvey, Paul. "On Board Shell's Prelude Barge, the World's Biggest Vessel." The Australian, March 4, 2017. http://www.theaustralian.com.au/business/mining-energy/on-board-shells-prelude-barge-the-worlds-biggest-vessel/news-story/61c10673c87ea2be73b671cd2984cf2c.

Kraemer, Susan. "Why Now Is the Time for Nuclear Cargo Shipping." Clean Technica, January 28, 2017. https://cleantechnica.com/2017/01/28/now-time-nuclear-cargo-shipping.

Kremer, William. "How Much Bigger Can Container Ships Get?" BBC News, February 19, 2013. http://www.bbc.com/news/magazine-21432226.

Machan, Teresa. "Cruising: New Innovations and Experiences for the 21st Century. *Telegraph*, April 4, 2014. http://www.telegraph.co.uk/travel/cruises/articles/Cruising-but-not-as-you-know-it-how-to-set-sail-in-the-21st-century.

Maxey, Kyle. "The Prelude FLNG Is Huge, But Is It a Ship?" Engineering.com, November 4, 2014. http://www.engineering.com/DesignerEdge/DesignerEdgeArticles/ArticleID/8864/The-Prelude-FLNG-is-Huge-but-Is-It-a-Ship.aspx.

Ryszka-Onions, Allan. *Ocean Ships*. Addlestone/Surrey, UK: Ian Allen Publishing, 2016.

Sharda. "The TI Class Super Tankers: The Fantastic Four." Marine Insight, July 22, 2016. https://www.marineinsight.com/types-of-ships/the-ti-class-super-tankers-the-fantastic-four.

Sloan, Gene. "Largest Cruise Ship Ever Sets Sail on Inaugural Voyage." *USAToday*, May 22, 2016. https://www.usatoday.com/story/travel/cruises/2016/05/22/royal-caribbean-harmony-inaugural-voyage/84739466.

Toto, Serkan. "NYK Super Eco Ship 2030: How Ships Will Look Like in the Future." Techcrunch.com, May 13, 2009. https://techcrunch.com/2009/05/13/nyk-super-eco-ship-2030-how-ships-will-look-like-in-the-future.

Ward, Peter. "The Evolution of the Oil Tanker." Eniday.com. Retrieved September 29, 2017. https://www.eniday.com/en/sparks_en/oil-tanker-future.

Wetzel, Gary. "America's New $13 Billion Aircraft Carrier Is Still Far from Ready." Foxtrot Alpha/Jalopnik, July 22, 2017. https://foxtrotalpha.jalopnik.com/americas-new-13-billion-aircraft-carrier-is-still-far-1797119016.

GLOSSARY

accommodate To fit or make room for.

ballast tank The compartment in a ship that takes in and discharges excess water to balance the ship.

bow The forward part of a boat or ship or its hull.

buoyancy The tendency or ability of something to float in water (or air).

containerization The development and use of cargo containers in shipping.

deadweight tonnage (DWT) The measure of total mass a ship can carry, excluding the weight of the ship itself.

drag The tendency of water to slow down objects or vehicles moving across its surface.

gross tonnage The measure of total capacity of a ship, especially a cargo ship or tanker.

hull The watertight body of a boat or ship.

keel The part of a ship or boat, sometimes finlike, that extends along its bottom to provide stability in the water.

knot A measure of a boat's or ship's speed on the water.

maiden voyage The first official journey of a boat or ship.

maritime Of or relating to the sea or ocean.

stern The back or rear-most part of a ship or boat.

upthrust The pushback an object in water experiences from the water around it.

FURTHER READING

Books

Bowman, Chris. *Monster Ships*. Minneapolis, MN: Bellwether Media, 2014.

Meister, Cari. *Ships*. Minneapolis, MN: Bullfrog Books, 2014.

Snashall, Sarah. *Spectacular Ships*. New York, NY: Kingfisher, 2016.

West, David. *Ships*. Mankato, MN: Smart Apple Media, 2016.

Websites

Engineering for Kids

engineeringforkids.com/programs/junior

A clearinghouse for websites geared toward young people interested in engineering.

The National Maritime Historical Society

www.seahistory.org/education/neat-stuff-kids

A kids' resource page from the National Maritime Historical Society.

INDEX

A
Archimedes, 12

B
ballasts, 31, 42
buoyancy, 11, 12–13

C
computer-aided design (CAD), 8
corrosion, 10–11

D
deadweight tonnage (DWT), 24
drag, 26

E
engineering, 8, 20, 32, 37, 39, 42
engines, 18–19, 20, 26, 31, 39
Exxon Valdez, 23

F
future shipping technologies, 26, 31, 36, 40–41

G
global economy, 27, 29
green technology, 20, 37–40

H
Harmony of the Seas, 5–6, 18–20
hull, 11, 18, 20, 23, 39, 42

L
liquefied natural gas, 26, 39

N
naval architects, 8, 24, 37, 39, 42
nuclear power, 40

S
seaworthiness, 8, 11
shipbuilding, 8–11
ships
    aircraft carrier, 32
    biggest on Earth, 27, 29–31
    container/cargo, 12, 27, 29–31, 34, 39
    cruise, 5, 6, 7, 12, 14–15, 18–20, 42
    military, 5, 32–36
    naval destroyers, 34–36
    ocean liners, 14–15
    tankers, 12, 21–24, 26
    warships, 12, 36
shipyards, 10, 41
solar power, 37–38
speed, 15, 18, 26, 31, 38
supertankers, 11, 24

T
Titanic, 11, 21